HEADSTRONG HALLIE!

The Story of Hallie Morse Daggett, the First Female "Fire Guard"

Written by Aimée Bissonette and Illustrated by David Hohn

PUBLISHED BY SLEEPING BEAR PRESS

Hallie leapt from her bed and raced to the window, pulling back the curtains. A bright orange glow filled the sky.

Flames licked the tops of far-off trees. Hallie's house was safe for now, but the winds could shift at any moment. Even if her home was safe, the forest was in danger—the trees, the animals, her neighbors.

Hallie raced to get dressed. She had to wake her sister, Leslie.

The fire crews would be here soon. They had to be ready. Hallie had to help save her forest home.

Hallie Morse Daggett
never feared the forest.

Certainly not!

She hiked among the tall trees of California's Siskiyou Mountains, listened for the calls of familiar birds, and looked for signs of wildlife. She fished the rushing Salmon River with her brother, Ben, and sister, Leslie.

She was an expert shot who loved to hunt.

There was really only one thing Hallie feared.

Fire. And summer was the worst time of all for forest fires.

Hallie had seen the horrible power of fire race through the trees, leaving them scorched and leafless. She had seen the animals of the forest scatter and flee from racing flames—deer and foxes, rabbits and tiny mice. And she had seen those flames come dangerously close to her family's home.

So whenever US Forest Service crews came to fight the fires, Hallie joined the fight. She and Leslie stamped out abandoned campfires. They brought food and supplies to the men at the fire line.

Fire was a constant worry in Hallie's life.

At night in bed, with the smell of smoke thick in the air, Hallie vowed to do more. Who knew the mountains better than she did? Who would protect them and keep her friends and family safe? Hallie decided she would work for the US Forest Service when she grew up.

What kind of girl dreams a dream like that?
A headstrong girl, for sure.

When Hallie and Leslie were older, they went to boarding school in San Francisco. School was fine, but city life was not for Hallie. Frilly dresses and feathered hats were not her style. She craved the smell of fir trees and wooded trails. She missed the roar of the Salmon River.

As soon as she finished school, Hallie began mailing letters to the US Forest Service. She wanted work. She wanted to help fight fires.

But the Forest Service said no.

A few years later, tragedy struck. The Great Fire of 1910 burned millions of acres of forest in Washington, Idaho, and Montana. Fanned by hurricane-force winds, the fire destroyed entire towns. People died—most of them firefighters.

Hallie was more determined than ever. She wrote more letters. The Forest Service needed someone like Hallie, she told them. She had grown up in the mountains. She knew forest fires and the dangers they posed. She simply would not take no for an answer.

But *no* was always the answer she got. The Forest Service didn't hire women.

In 1913, Hallie finally got her break. The man who was the fire lookout at the Eddy Gulch Lookout Station quit to take a better paying job—right before the start of fire season. Hallie knew the Forest Service would act quickly to fill the post. She sat down and wrote her most heartfelt letter yet.

Ranger M. H. McCarthy received three applications for the Eddy Gulch fire lookout job. In addition to Hallie, two men applied. Ranger McCarthy carefully reviewed all three applications, then sent his recommendation to his boss:

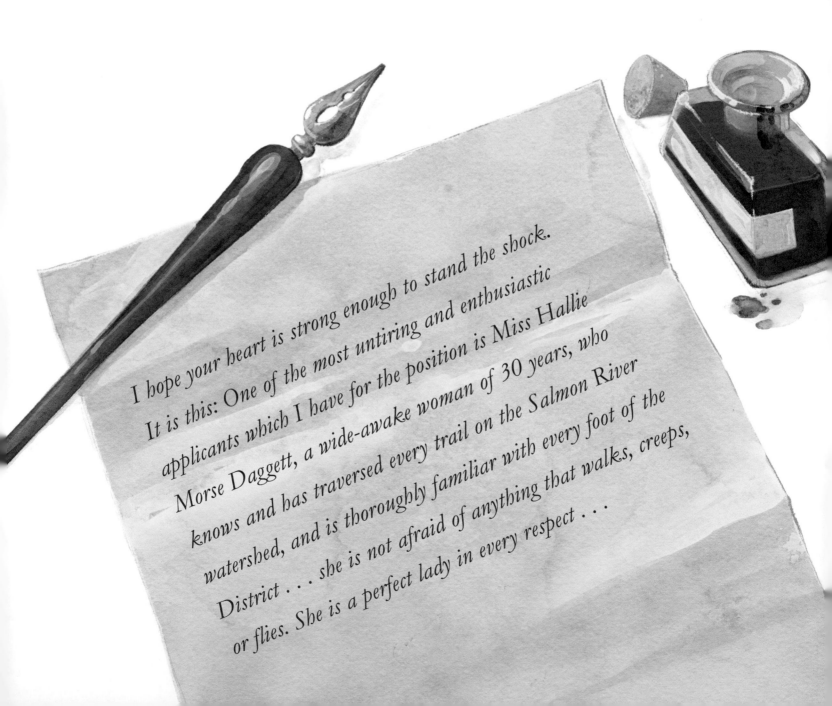

I hope your heart is strong enough to stand the shock. It is this: One of the most untiring and enthusiastic applicants which I have for the position is Miss Hallie Morse Daggett, a wide-awake woman of 30 years, who knows and has traversed every trail on the Salmon River watershed, and is thoroughly familiar with every foot of the District . . . she is not afraid of anything that walks, creeps, or flies. She is a perfect lady in every respect . . .

Hallie got the job!

News spread that Hallie would be the new lookout at Eddy Gulch. It caused quite a stir.

Some of the Forest Service men made bets she would quit within a few days. They were sure Hallie would be frightened by the fierce electrical storms atop the mountain. They were sure she would be lonely at the isolated station where days or even weeks could pass without seeing another human being.

They didn't know Hallie.

Hallie loved the tiny lookout cabin from the first time she saw it.

The Eddy Gulch station was on top of the peak that overlooked Hallie's girlhood home. The view from the cabin took Hallie's breath away. To the east was magnificent Mount Shasta—at more than 14,000 feet high. To the west, the Pacific Ocean.

Hallie's cabin became home to pet chipmunks that ate out of her hand and raided her pockets for corn or biscuits. A pair of porcupines made their way into the cabin each night, too, no matter what Hallie did to keep them out.

There were larger animals such as bears and coyotes in the area, too. One morning, Hallie discovered a large panther track out on the trail. Hallie started wearing her gun out on her walks after that.

Hallie loved her fire lookout work.

Each morning, Hallie raised the American flag. She gathered firewood and fetched water from a nearby spring. Sometimes a hunter, camper, or fellow forest guard would come by to visit.

And Leslie made the three-hour climb up the mountain on horseback every week to bring Hallie newspapers, supplies, and letters from home.

By day, Hallie watched for smoke.

At night, she watched for the red glare of fire, which she described as "red stars in the blue-black background of moonless nights." Three times a day Hallie telephoned Ranger McCarthy from the pole-mounted telephone outside her cabin—more often if she spotted smoke or flame.

In her first season on the job, Hallie spotted forty fires. Because of her quick reporting, fewer than five acres of forest burned.

Hallie worked the 1913 fire season at the Eddy Gulch Lookout Station and for fourteen more seasons after that.

She arrived every spring when it was still so cold that the streams were frozen over and Hallie had no source of water. Hallie used shovels to fetch snow to melt instead.

She stayed until late fall when the snow fell again and there was no longer a fire danger.

When fire season ended and it was time to make her way back down the mountain, Hallie faced her return to "Civilization" with sadness.

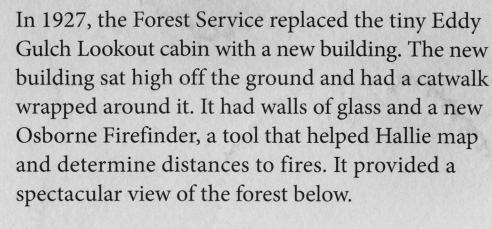

In 1927, the Forest Service replaced the tiny Eddy Gulch Lookout cabin with a new building. The new building sat high off the ground and had a catwalk wrapped around it. It had walls of glass and a new Osborne Firefinder, a tool that helped Hallie map and determine distances to fires. It provided a spectacular view of the forest below.

But to Hallie, the new lookout station no longer felt like home. It was no more her style than the frilly dresses and feathered hats she had worn at boarding school.

Hallie's first season in the new building was her last.

Hallie retired in 1927 with no regrets. From the time she was little, she had dreamed of a life where she would protect the mountains and forests she loved. She knew what she wanted and she followed her heart—even when that meant doing things others wouldn't or didn't want to do.

And in the end, she found a place in the world that was just right for her.

What kind of girl dreams a dream like that?
A wonderfully headstrong one, for sure.

AUTHOR'S NOTE

Most of what we know about Hallie is from newspaper articles and a handful of photographs from her early years. Hallie lived alone for months upon months. There are many details of her day-to-day life we simply don't know, which means there are some questions we cannot answer. For instance, although Hallie is quoted in one early article as saying she did not own a dog or feel the need for one, dogs can be seen in nearly every photograph we have of her at the lookout station. Did the dogs belong to someone else? Did Hallie change her mind after a few years on the mountain?

We do know that when Hallie was hired by the US Forest Service, she was its first woman "fire guard." She was paid $840 per year for up to seven months of round-the-clock work. Hiring Hallie was an experiment, but she quickly proved her worth. Ranger M. H. McCarthy praised Hallie's work her first summer on the job when only five acres of forest burned under her watch, saying, "Had one less faithful been on the Lookout, it might easily have been five thousand." And because she appreciated the opportunity, Hallie was determined not to let Ranger McCarthy down. Hallie is quoted as saying she knew she had to do well "for I knew that the appointment

of a woman was rather in the nature of an experiment, and naturally felt that there was a great deal due the men who had been willing to give me the chance."

We also know there was plenty of danger in Hallie's work. The electrical storms were intense. They lit up the sky and rattled the walls of Hallie's cabin. The threat of wild animals was real, too. During one of her first seasons at the lookout station, Hallie had to kill a bear, four wildcats, and three coyotes.

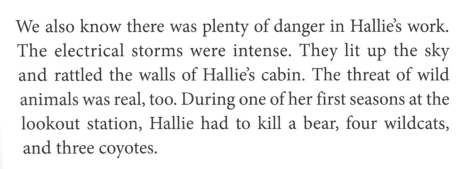

Hallie never married or had children. Protecting the forest, its animals, and the people who lived there was her life's work. Even after she retired from the US Forest Service, she stayed in her beloved Siskiyou Mountains, moving first to a home about 10 miles

from Eddy Gulch and then later to the town of Etna, California, to be near her sister, Leslie.

Hallie lived to see the US Forest Service expand its ranks to include many women in field positions, which undoubtedly made her happy. She died in 1964 at the age of 85. Her home in Etna was donated to the city after her death and thereafter was moved to the city park. It is now a historical interpretive site where visitors can learn more about Hallie and her US Forest Service work.

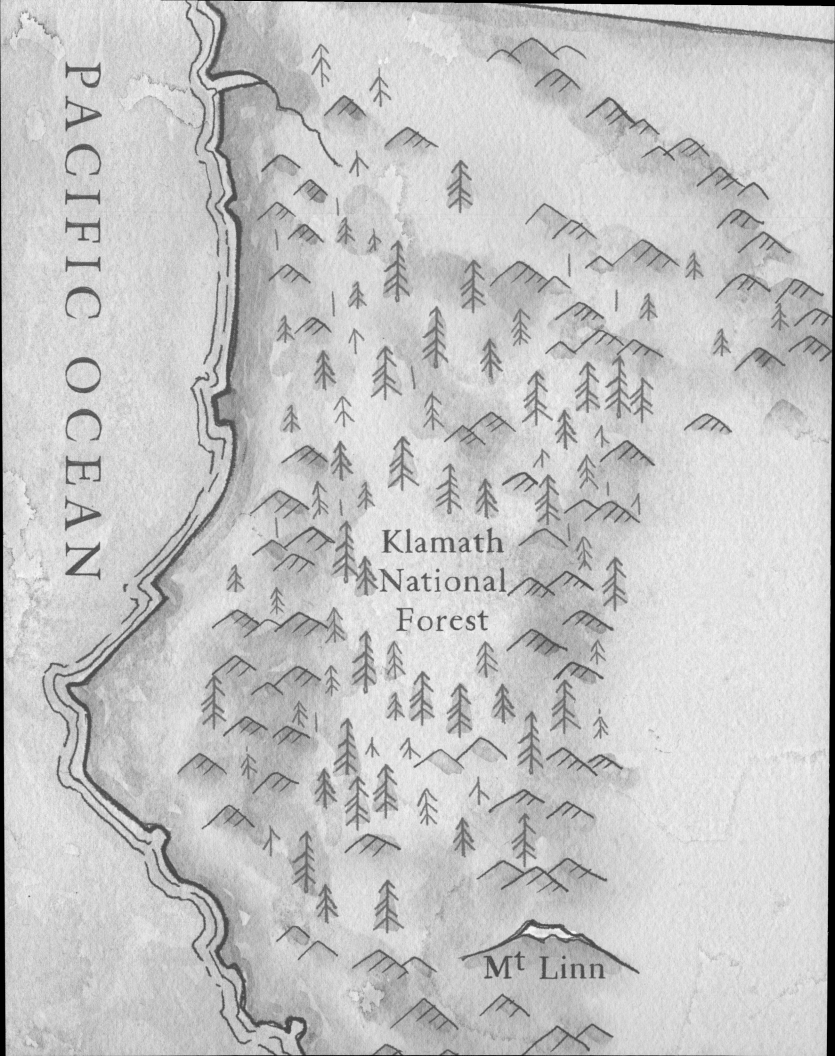